X GAMES

Skateboarding Street

GAMES

by Connie Colwell Miller

Reading Consultant:
Barbara J. Fox
Reading Specialist
North Carolina State University

Content Consultant:
Ben Hobson
Content Coordinator
Extreme Sports Channel
United Kingdom

Capstone
press

Mankato, Minnesota

Blazers is published by Capstone Press,
151 Good Counsel Drive, P.O. Box 669, Mankato, Minnesota 56002.
www.capstonepress.com

Library of Congress Cataloging-in-Publication Data
Miller, Connie Colwell, 1976–
    Skateboarding Street / by Connie Colwell Miller.
    p. cm. — (Blazers. X games)
    Summary: "Describes the X Games street skating event, including the course,
how the event is judged, tricks, and star skaters" — Provided by publisher.
    Includes bibliographical references and index.
    ISBN-13: 978-1-4296-1291-3 (hardcover)
    ISBN-10: 1-4296-1291-6 (hardcover)
    1. Skateboarding. I. Title. II. Series.
GV859.8.M554 2008
796.22 — dc22   2007032826

Essential content terms are bold and are defined at the bottom of the page where they first appear.

Editorial Credits
Carrie A. Braulick and Abby Czeskleba, editors; Bobbi J. Wyss, set designer;
    Alison Thiele, designer; Jo Miller, photo researcher

Photo Credits
AP Images/Kevork Djansezian, 23, 27; Mark J. Terrill, 13;
    Newport Daily News/Dave Hansen, cover; Reed Saxon, 5, 9
Corbis/Bo Bridges, 28–29
Getty Images Inc./WireImage/Chris Polk, 20–21; Mike Ehrmann, 7, 8
SportsChrome, Inc/Mike Ehrmann, 17
ZUMA Press/Icon SMI/Tony Donaldson, 11, 12, 14–15, 19, 24

1 2 3 4 5 6 13 12 11 10 09 08

Table Of Contents

Airwalking to a Win

Excited skateboarding fans watched with wonder at the X Games on August 4, 2006. Chris Cole was in the middle of a great **run**.

run (RUHN) — a skater's turn on the course

Chris Cole

Cole was doing **airwalks** and other amazing tricks. The crowd was loving every second of Cole's run.

airwalk (AIR-wawk) — a trick done in midair; skaters "walk" by moving their legs back and forth.

BLAZER FACT

Chris Cole started skating when he was 8 years old.

Cole did a backside 360 **kickflip** over the

stairs. The crowd went wild when he landed.

The exciting run earned him the gold medal.

kickflip (KIK-flip) — a trick in which the skater flips
the board one to three times while it is in the air

Street Basics

In skateboarding street, skaters jump over **obstacles** like steps and ledges. Skaters also use obstacles to do grinds and other wild tricks.

obstacle (OB-stuh-kuhl) — something a skater jumps or rides over

grind

11

Sometimes, skaters compete on streets. Other times, competitions take place on courses built just for the event.

obstacle

Street Course Diagram

quarterpipe

kicker

rail

Going for the Gold

Skaters show off their best moves at the X Games. The 20 men perform in three **sessions**. Only 10 skaters make it to the final. Eight skaters perform in the women's final. Men and women compete in different finals.

session (SESH-uhn) — a round of skateboarding

17

Skaters perform three sessions during the final round. The six judges score skaters for each session. Skaters drop the highest and lowest score from each session. Skaters receive a final score based on their **average** number of points.

average (AV-uh-rij) — a number found by adding all scores together and dividing by the number of scores

BLAZER FACT

Judges reward scores from zero to 100 points for each session.

The skater with the highest score wins the gold medal. The second and third place skaters also earn medals for their amazing moves.

Stars of Street

Star street skaters battle every year for a spot at the X Games. Ryan Sheckler, Andrew Reynolds, and Elissa Steamer are some of the best skaters. They practice nonstop for a chance to compete.

Elissa Steamer

Paul Rodriguez

Paul Rodriguez won the gold medal at the X Games in 2004 and 2005. He became the first skater to win two years in a row in the men's competition. Rodriguez is known for landing difficult tricks time after time.

BLAZER FACT

Paul Rodriguez's nickname is "P-Rod."

The best skaters amaze fans with new tricks. Fans can expect more thrills as street skaters roll their way to the top.

BLAZER FACT

A skater who invents a trick gets to name it.

A Perfect Grind!

Glossary

airwalk (AIR-wawk) — a trick done in midair; skaters "walk" by moving their legs back and forth.

average (AV-uh-rij) — a number found by adding all scores together and dividing by the number of scores

competition (kahm-puh-TI-shuhn) — a contest between two or more people

grind (GRINDE) — a trick in which the skater rides on top of a metal obstacle; named after the sound the skateboard makes when it rubs against the metal.

invent (in-VENT) — to think up or create something new

kickflip (KIK-flip) — a trick in which the skater flips the board one to three times while it is in the air

obstacle (OB-stuh-kuhl) — something a skater jumps or rides over

run (RUHN) — a skater's turn on the course

session (SESH-uhn) — a round of skateboarding

Read More

Hocking, Justin. *Famous Skateboarders.* Power Skateboarding. New York: PowerKids Press, 2006.

Murdico, Suzanne J. *Skateboarding in the X Games.* The World of Skateboarding. New York: Rosen, 2003.

Savage, Jeff. *Street Skating: Grinds and Grabs.* Skateboarding. Mankato, Minn.: Capstone Press, 2005.

Internet Sites

FactHound offers a safe, fun way to find Internet sites related to this book. All of the sites on FactHound have been researched by our staff.

Here's how:
1. Visit *www.facthound.com*
2. Choose your grade level.
3. Type in this book ID **1429612916** for age-appropriate sites. You may also browse subjects by clicking on letters, or by clicking on pictures and words.
4. Click on the **Fetch It** button.

FactHound will fetch the best sites for you!

Index